STD

ACPL ITEM
DISCARDED

P9-AFY-918

A CLOSE LOOK
AT THE MOON

A CLOSE LOOK AT THE MOON

G. Jeffrey Taylor

Illustrated with photographs and drawings

DODD, MEAD & COMPANY · NEW YORK

ILLUSTRATION CREDITS:

Fred Hörz (NASA, Johnson Space Center), 70; Lick Observatory, 24, 30 (bottom); William Mansker, 57 (top); G. Jeffrey Taylor, 71, 72; John A. Wood (Smithsonian Astrophysical Observatory), 68, 69. All other photographs are from the National Aeronautics and Space Administration (provided by the National Space Science Data Center and the Office of Public Affairs of the Johnson Space Center).
Drawings on pages 15, 61, 74, 76, 79, 80, and 90 are by Todd Pink.

Copyright © 1980 by G. Jeffrey Taylor
All rights reserved
No part of this book may be reproduced in any form
without permission in writing from the publisher
Printed in the United States of America

1   2   3   4   5   6   7   8   9   10

Library of Congress Cataloging in Publication Data

Taylor, G   Jeffrey date
    A close look at the moon.

    Includes index.
    SUMMARY: Discusses the origins, terrain, and
atmosphere of the moon as revealed in recent discoveries.
    1. Moon—Juvenile literature.   [1. Moon]
I. Title.
QB582.T38   559.9′1   79-24721
ISBN 0-396-07797-8

For Sally T. Montoya—the best teacher

2090208

Contents

Apollo 11 astronaut "Buzz" Aldrin stepping off lunar module to become the second person to walk on the moon.

1. Astronauts on the Moon

The moon appears as the largest and brightest object in the night sky. For thousands of years people have looked up at it and wondered how it got there and what it is made of. For a long time, everyone had to look with unaided eyes. Then in 1610, an Italian scientist named Galileo aimed a telescope—one of the first ever built—at the moon. Suddenly, the world had a whole new way of studying this little planet. Instead of the moon being a round object that has vague light and dark areas, it became a place that has mountains and lowlands, rough areas and smooth areas.

As the years passed, telescopes were improved and scientists learned more about the moon. Then in 1959, we took another giant step in the study of the moon. An unmanned Russian space-craft named Luna 3 traveled around the moon, took pictures, and radioed them back to earth. Luna 3 gave scientists their first look at the farside of the moon. (The moon always keeps the same side toward the earth, so no one had ever seen the other side.)

Other unmanned spacecraft followed during the next ten years. They produced thousands of sharp photographs of the moon, giving scientists a much better look than even the largest telescopes had given them. But scientists were still limited in what they could conclude about the moon. They knew what it *looked* like, but they could not determine what it was *made* of.

All that changed on July 20, 1969. Neil Armstrong and Edwin ("Buzz") Aldrin landed a spacecraft, nicknamed *Eagle*, on a relatively smooth area of the moon called the Sea of Tranquillity.

"Tranquillity Base here, Houston," Armstrong said. "The *Eagle* has landed."

Armstrong and Aldrin soon put on bulky space suits and climbed out of the *Eagle*. They spent slightly more than two hours on the moon's surface and collected 48 pounds (22 kilograms) of rock and dirt. They packed the samples in special containers and stowed them in their spacecraft for the return trip to earth.

It was a remarkable achievement and it opened up an entirely new way to study the moon. Instead of looking at the earth's nearest planetary neighbor, scientists could study pieces of it. We could finally determine what the moon is made of.

The first mission to land on the moon was named Apollo 11. It was followed by five other manned landings named Apollo 12, 14, 15, 16, and 17. (Apollo 13 planned to land, too, but equipment trouble prevented it from landing on the moon.) Each mission stayed longer on the moon and collected more rock samples than the mission before it. Whereas the Apollo 11 astronauts spent only a little over two hours working on the moon's

Apollo 14 astronaut Alan Shepard stands by the flag. Shadows are from the lunar module (left), astronaut Ed Mitchell (center), and the antenna (right) used to radio the astronauts' conversations back to earth.

A view of the moon that we cannot see from the earth. Most of the left side of this photograph, which was taken from an Apollo spacecraft circling the moon, is of the side of the moon that never faces the earth.

surface and collected only 48 pounds of rock and soil, the Apollo 17 astronauts spent a total of 22 hours (divided into three separate sessions) and collected 243 pounds (110 kilograms) of samples. All the missions combined brought back a total of 838 pounds (381 kilograms) of rock and soil.

Spacecraft sent by Russian scientists also returned samples from three places on the moon. These were unpiloted, automated spacecraft that brought back small amounts of moon soil. The first Russian spacecraft to return a sample was called Luna 16. It brought back 3½ ounces (100 grams) of soil. Luna 20 returned only about one ounce (30 grams), and Luna 24 collected six ounces (170 grams) of moon soil.

Although these automated spacecraft returned small amounts of soil compared to the amounts brought back by the Apollo missions, the samples were interesting and useful to scientists because the Luna spacecraft landed in places not visited by Apollo astronauts. Scientists think it is important to collect samples from as many places as possible to be sure that we discover all the types of rocks found on the moon.

This book describes what the geologists and other scientists found when they studied the rocks brought back by the Apollo astronauts and by the Luna spacecraft. It also compares the moon to our home planet, earth, and shows how scientists have discovered a lot about the earth by studying rocks from the moon.

2. Basic Facts About the Moon

Long before Apollo astronauts traveled through space, scientists knew a great many facts about the moon.

One fact is that the moon is a *satellite* of the earth. That is, it follows a circular path, or orbit, around the earth. Each orbit takes 27 days. Most of the other planets have satellites, too. The planet Jupiter, in fact, has 12 satellites, or moons, around it.

The distance from the earth to the moon is about 238,000 miles (382,000 kilometers). That makes the moon our closest neighbor in space. The next nearest neighbor is the planet Venus, which is never closer than 25 million miles (40 million kilometers).

As everyone knows, the moon usually does not appear as a full circle in the sky. Sometimes only half is visible, other times only a thin sliver. On one day each month, we cannot see the moon at all. This disappearing act is caused by the moon's motion around the earth.

Both earth and moon are lighted by light coming from the sun. Neither gives off any light of its own. The sun shines on half the moon (and also on half the earth) all the time. When that half of the moon is visible from the earth, we see a full moon. This occurs when the earth is between the sun and the moon. But when the moon is between the sun and the earth, we view only the unlighted half of the moon, which means that we cannot see it at all. In between these positions we see some of the moon, but not all of it.

Although the moon takes 27 days to make its trip around the earth, the time from one full moon to the next is 29½ days. The extra time arises because of the earth's motion around the sun. This motion changes the angle at which the sun shines on the

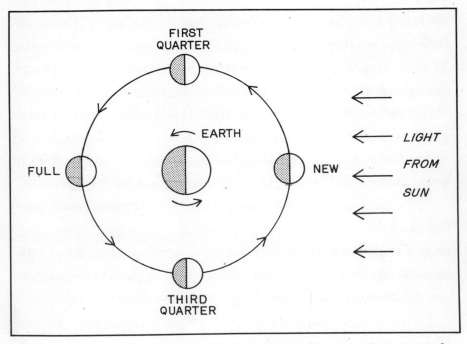

We usually do not see the entire lighted half of the moon because of the moon's motion around the earth.

moon and so it takes a little extra time for the moon, earth, and sun to be lined up again.

Another interesting fact about the moon is that it always keeps the same side toward the earth. Scientists refer to the side facing us as the "nearside" or "earth-facing side" of the moon. They call the other side the "farside." This results from the moon taking exactly the same length of time to spin once, about 27 days, as it takes to travel once around the earth.

Because the moon takes 27 days to turn once, daytime and nighttime on the moon each lasts almost two weeks. A particular spot on the moon is illuminated by the sun for about half (13½ days) of each 27-day period. The same spot is in darkness for the other half. As a result, daytime and nighttime on the moon each lasts 13½ days.

The moon, like the earth, is shaped like a round ball, or sphere. Scientists knew that the distance from the surface to the center, the radius of the sphere, is 1,090 miles (1,738 kilometers). This is a fairly big ball, but it is only one-fourth the size of the earth.

The moon weighs 180 billion trillion pounds (75 billion trillion kilograms). It may sound like a lot, but it is small compared to the planets. The earth, for example, weighs 80 times more than the moon does.

The smaller weight of the moon causes the pull of gravity to be weaker on it. Gravity is one of the forces in nature that attracts one object to another. Other forces are magnetism and electricity.

Right: *For the same reason that we on earth do not usually see a full moon, visitors to the moon do not usually see a "full earth."*

Just as a magnet attracts an iron needle or a nail to it, the *mass* of one object attracts the mass of another. If you have two bags the same size and fill one with rocks and the other with feathers, the one containing the rocks will be heavier because it has more mass.

The large mass of the earth attracts each of us to it. As a result, when we jump up we do not keep going higher and higher. We fall back down. But the moon has a smaller mass than the earth, so the pull of gravity is weaker. You would not, therefore, weigh as much on the moon as you do on the earth. If you weigh 78 pounds (36 kilograms) here, you would weigh only 13 pounds (6 kilograms) on the moon.

The lower gravity could be fun. If you can hit a baseball 400 feet (120 meters) on earth, like home run king Hank Aaron, you could belt the ball a half mile (750 meters) on the moon! And think of how far you could kick a soccer ball.

The only problem with the moon's low gravity is that it prevented air from accumulating on the moon. The earth's atmosphere formed when gases seeped out of the interior and collected in a layer surrounding the planet. Although some of the gases escaped into space, the earth's strong gravity held most of them in this layer, which we call the atmosphere. The gases were brought up mixed with molten rock, or lava, and escaped from the lava and entered the atmosphere during volcanic eruptions. (An exception is the gas oxygen. Most of this gas was formed by plants during a period of billions of years. Plants use a gas called carbon dioxide and convert it to oxygen.)

On the moon, the gases that came to the surface with volcanic lava floated off into space because the moon's gravity was too weak to hold them. You cannot, therefore, breathe on the moon, unless you bring air with you. The astronauts wore airtight space suits and carried their air in containers on their backs, somewhat like underwater divers do here on earth.

The lack of air on the moon not only makes it impossible to breathe without a space suit. It also prevents moonwalkers from seeing red, orange, and pink sunsets because such colorful displays occur only where there is enough air around to bend the light from the sun. On the moon, the sun disappears behind the horizon and it becomes dark immediately. It is either daytime or nighttime, never in between as it is during twilight on the earth.

If an astronaut on the moon walks into the shadow of a large boulder, he finds that the shadow is totally dark. That does not happen on the earth, where some light appears in even the darkest of shadows because atoms and dust particles in the air scatter the light. There is no air on the moon, so the shadows are very dark.

Not having a protective cushion of air around them also creates some problems for visitors to the moon. They are not protected from falling meteorites or from the dangerous X-rays, gamma rays, and cosmic rays that come from the sun and other parts of space.

The earth's atmosphere guards us from these hazards. Although meteorites do fall to the ground on earth, they are almost always slowed down as they travel through the air. A meteorite even decreases in size during its trip through the atmosphere because it heats up and begins to vaporize (become a gas) on the outside as the air pushes against it. The smallest meteorites burn up completely.

19

Astronaut Jack Schmitt collecting rock samples on the moon. The lack of air on the moon causes the shadows made by the large boulder and the dune-buggy, or Rover, to be totally dark. The upside-down umbrella is a radio antenna that allows the astronaut to talk to scientists back on earth.

Only rarely does a large meteorite hit the earth going full speed—about 10 miles per second (15 kilometers per second). When this happens, a crater forms where the meteorite hits. This occurred in Arizona less than 50,000 years ago and now a crater about three-fourths of a mile (one kilometer) across marks the spot. Fortunately, such large meteorites do not crash into the earth very often—once every 50,000 years or so.

But on the moon, even the tiniest meteorites whack into the surface traveling full speed. And they all make craters, although some of the craters are miniature in size.

The air above us also absorbs the harmful radiation in the form of X-rays, gamma rays, and cosmic rays coming at us from space. This radiation comes from the sun and from distant parts of space where stars have exploded. If someone wanted to live on the moon, he would need to build a thick shelter to protect himself. The space suits worn by the astronauts did not actually provide much protection, but the astronauts were exposed for too short a time for the radiation to do any damage: The longest time spent working on the moon's surface was only 22 hours by Apollo 17 astronauts Eugene Cernan and Harrison Schmitt.

Temperatures on the moon are both much hotter and much colder than on earth. On earth, the temperature may reach 100°F (38°C) on a hot summer day, and cool to 70°F (21°C) at night. Or it may be 10°F (−12°C) during a cold winter day, followed by −10°F (−23°C) at night. But the moon's surface reaches a scorching 270°F (134°C) during the daytime and cools to a frigid −270°F (−170°C) at night.

These extreme temperatures also result from the absence of an atmosphere on the moon. During the moon's daytime, the sun shines directly onto the surface. With no atmosphere to absorb some of the heat and to move it around in winds, which is what happens on the earth, the temperature of the rocks on the moon's

21

surface becomes quite hot. At nighttime here on earth, much of the warmth the planet received from the sun during the daytime is transferred from the ground to the air. As the ground loses heat after the sun sets, the air receives it. But on the moon, the surface cools off by losing heat directly into space.

3. A Distant View of the Moon

The geologic study of the moon began in 1610 when Galileo peered at the moon through a homemade telescope. Galileo was not the first person to make a telescope, but he was the first to point it toward the sky and examine the moon, planets, and stars. Scientists have studied the moon ever since, first with telescopes, then with automated spacecraft that circled the moon, took pictures and radioed them back to earth. The long hours that scientists have spent looking through telescopes and examining photographs have revealed much about the moon—even before astronauts began collecting pieces of the moon for scientists to study up close, instead of from thousands of miles away.

Smooth Lowlands and Rugged Highlands
As we all know from our own moongazing, the moon has lighter and darker areas. The pattern made up by these light and dark patches resembles a face—the "Man in the Moon." When Galileo looked through his telescope, he saw that the dark areas were smoother and appeared to be lower than the lighter areas, which

The moon has light and dark areas, and numerous craters. This photo-graph was taken through a telescope at Lick Observatory in California.

were higher and much more rugged. Galileo thought that the dark areas might be oceans, so he named them *maria*, which is the Latin word for "seas." (Maria is pronounced MAH-ree-ah. For one "sea," the word is *mare*, pronounced MAH-ray, which rhymes with sorry.) Although scientists now know that the

View seen by Apollo 17 astronauts as they flew around the moon. The maria are smoother and lower than the highlands. The larger crater in the upper left is about 12 miles (20 kilometers) across.

maria are not really seas, we still use the word.

Galileo called the rough, lighter areas *terra*, the Latin word for "land." This word is also still used, but most scientists prefer to say "highlands" or "uplands."

Most of the large features on the moon's nearside were named in 1651 by Johannes Riccioli, an Italian Jesuit priest. He used a map made by his student, Francesco Grimaldi. Riccioli gave the maria a variety of imaginative names and, depending on their sizes, called them oceans, seas, bays, or lakes.

Since Riccioli's work, moon maps display names like Oceanus Procellarum (Ocean of Storms), Mare Serenitatis (Sea of Serenity), Mare Tranquillitatis (Sea of Tranquillity), Sinus Iridium (Bay of Rainbows), and Lacus Somniorum (Lake of Dreams). He even named one area—the region where Apollo 15 would land 320 years later—the Marsh of Decay.

Riccioli and Grimaldi honored famous scientists and philosophers by naming the giant holes, or craters, visible on the moon after them. Some of these are Kepler, Plato, Copernicus, and Galileo. Somewhat immodestly, they even named two of the largest craters after themselves!

Almost all the mare areas are on the nearside on the moon. This was discovered when spacecraft flew around the moon and photographed the farside. A few mare areas are present, but most of the farside is light-colored, mountainous highlands.

Craters Everywhere

In addition to color, the most obvious difference between the maria and highlands is that the maria are much smoother than the rough, rocky highlands. Close inspection of the highlands shows that numerous circular holes cover the surface. These holes range in size from the smallest visible in photographs (about one yard) to hundreds of miles across. Scientists call these holes *craters*.

The craters are deep, too. Most are about one-fifth as deep as they are wide. A crater 10 miles (15 kilometers) across, therefore, is about 2 miles (3 kilometers) deep.

The crater Tsiolkovsky, 125 miles (200 kilometers) across, is one of the few areas on the farside that contains mare material.

Almost all the mountains in the highlands are the rims of large craters. And there are so many craters present that they seem to form on top of each other. In many cases, a crater in the highlands has been almost totally erased by other craters made in the same spot.

Although the maria are smoother than the highlands, they are not completely free of craters. There are, however, fewer craters than there are in the highlands.

How did all these craters form? Geologists know that craters are made in three main ways. One is by meteorites striking the surface. Craters formed in this way are called *impact craters.* Another is by the collapse of the top of a volcano. Geologists call this type of crater a *caldera.* A third way to make a crater is by the violent eruption of lava from a volcano.

By studying the appearance of all types of craters on the earth (and even by making small impact craters in special laboratories), scientists concluded that most of the craters on the moon have been formed by meteorites crashing into the moon's rocky surface.

Geologists discovered that impact craters have several features. One is that their rims rise above the surrounding ground. This occurs because the gigantic explosion that takes place when a fast-moving meteorite hits the ground throws rock out of the crater and dumps it nearby. Also, the layers of rock on the rim are pushed up and tilted. In fact, they are sometimes tilted upside down.

The walls of an impact crater are usually very steep. Sheer cliffs are common. On huge craters, the walls look like they have

Kepler, an impact crater on the moon, is 20 miles (32 kilometers) across. The rim rises above the surrounding plains.

Above: *The crater Tycho, 54 miles (87 kilometers) across, has a central uplift on its floor and steep stairs, or terraces, on its walls.*

Below: *Close-up view of Copernicus crater.*

Right: *The crater near the top of this picture is Copernicus, 57 miles (91 kilometers) across. Bright streaks, called rays, come from Copernicus and cross the smooth, dark surface of Mare Imbrium. The crater near the center of the photograph is called Pytheas and is 12 miles (19 kilometers) across.*

large stairs going up them. Geologists call these stairs *terraces*.

Many craters on the moon are surrounded by bright streaks called *rays*. The rays start near the crater and extend for distances far greater than the size of the crater. For instance, some rays from the crater Tycho, which is 54 miles (87 kilometers) across, stretch halfway around the moon.

Mountains occur in the centers of craters that are larger than 25 miles (40 kilometers) across. These mountains, called *central uplifts*, rise several hundred meters above the floor of the crater. Some geologists think that central uplifts practically jump up immediately after a crater forms, somewhat like the spurt of water you see when you drop a rock into a pond. Others think

Close-up view of Tsiolkovsky Crater, showing central uplift and dark mare material.

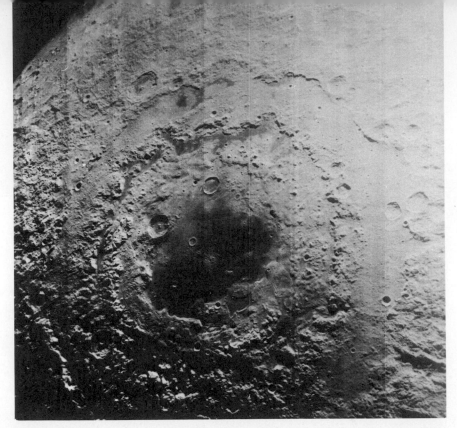

Gigantic impact crater called the Orientale Basin. The center is partially filled with mare material. The outer circular mountain chain makes a circle 560 miles (900 kilometers) across.

that the mountains rise up much more slowly. In this view, the mountains develop on the floor of the crater to make up for the great weight of the rock that was thrown out when the crater formed.

Some craters are so large and complicated that geologists call them *multi-ringed basins*, or just *basins* for short. There are 43 basins larger than 140 miles (220 kilometers) across. Most of the maria occur inside large basins.

The best example is the Orientale Basin. It occurs on the

33

moon's farside, just out of sight from earth. The basin has a smooth central area that is partly filled with mare material, and three circular mountain chains. The outer ring of mountains forms a circle 560 miles (900 kilometers) across—about the distance from Houston, Texas, to Memphis, Tennessee.

The Imbrium Basin (Mare Imbrium, the Sea of Rains) is even larger. Its inner ring of mountains is 440 miles (700 kilometers) across and its outer ring is 800 miles (1,300 kilometers) across. Such enormous craters must have formed when extremely large meteorites—up to a hundred kilometers (60 miles) across—struck the moon.

Volcanoes, Lava Flows, and Other Features

Before the Apollo moon landings, many geologists thought that the maria were made of lava flows. Many features that occur in the maria looked as if they were formed when lava (molten rock) flowed across the moon's surface. In many areas, long, curved cliffs occur. These cliffs, or *scarps* as geologists prefer to call them, are usually only 10 to 30 meters high and look like the fronts of lava flows.

Another interesting group of features that also formed by lava flowing downhill are *rilles*. These are long valleys that stretch across the surfaces of maria. Some are straight, but others make irregular, curved patterns. They look somewhat like rivers do

Lava flows in Mare Imbrium. The cliffs at the edges of the flows are about 80 feet (25 meters) high. You can also see wrinkle ridges in this picture. Dark, curved area on the right is part of the Apollo spacecraft.

2090208

A rille following a curved path across a mare, near the highlands. The crater in the center is about 3 miles (5 kilometers) across.

on earth. In fact, the resemblance led some scientists to suggest that the rilles were formed by water flowing in rivers on the moon.

Other scientists disagreed. They pointed out that rivers on earth become wider and deeper the farther they flow. The Mississippi River, for example, begins as small creeks in Minnesota and ends up as a wide, deep river in New Orleans. But rilles are just the opposite: The farther downhill they go, the narrower and shallower they become.

Most scientists now think that rilles formed as underground channels that carried hot lava. After the lava had flowed away, the tunnels that remained collapsed, forming a valley. The Apollo 15 astronauts landed next to a rille. Their observations and the studies of the rocks they returned support the lava-channel idea.

The mare surfaces also contain many narrow ridges, called *wrinkle ridges*. These are the opposite of rilles. Instead of being

Wrinkle ridges in the Ocean of Storms.

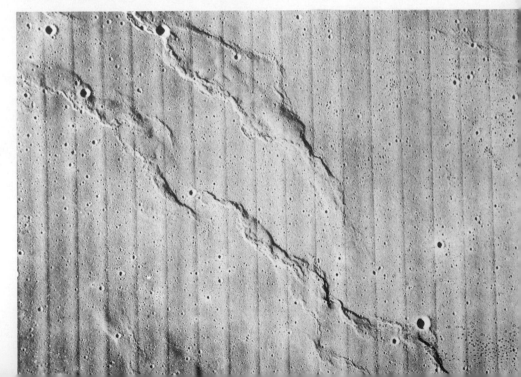

long valleys, wrinkle ridges are long, narrow high places.

Scientists are not sure how ridges formed, but they have plenty of ideas. One is that the ridges are places where lava came up from deeper in the moon and squeezed out, but did not flow very far. Another is that large areas of the maria were pushed up. The places between the push-up areas would be squeezed and might form the wrinkle ridges.

There are no active volcanoes on the moon. In fact, few mountains on the moon look like inactive volcanoes. One feature that seems to be a type of volcano, however, is a *dome*. Domes are low, circular, rounded hills. They are up to 10 miles (15 kilometers) across, but only 2,500 feet (750 meters) high.

Other features that probably formed during or after the erup-

Rilles and domes in the Ocean of Storms. The largest crater (located near the bottom of the photograph) is 6 miles (10 kilometers) across.

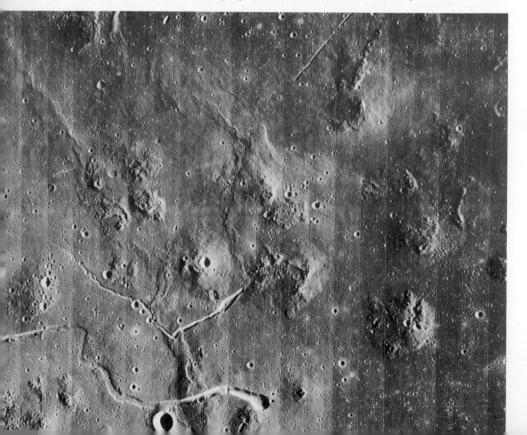

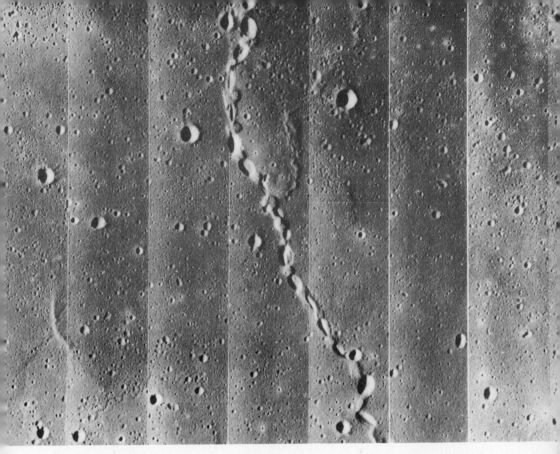

A chain of small craters in a mare. The craters are about half a mile (1 kilometer) across.

tion of lava are *cones* and *crater chains*. On the earth, cones form when a volcano erupts violently and sends up a dense cloud of hot dust (ash) and pebble-sized fragments (cinders). This material accumulates around the place where the eruption is taking place, and builds up a cone-shaped mountain. Cones probably formed the same way on the moon, but scientists find very few of them.

Groups of small craters lined up in a row or along a curved path also occur on the moon. Many of these groups, called crater chains, formed when underground lava channels collapsed. Crater chains like this, therefore, are probably incompletely formed rilles.

Other crater chains, especially those that lie along straight lines, may have formed when a group of large rocks were thrown out of an impact crater and landed in a row.

Questions and More Questions

Scientists knew a lot about the moon from their studies of its surface. They knew there were maria and highlands, craters everywhere, and some features formed during lava eruptions.

But many questions remained: What are the rocks made of? How old are they? Were there ever rivers? Is there water on the moon? Is the moon like the earth? Is there life on the moon?

These questions could be answered only by studying and analyzing pieces of the moon. The scientists needed to collect some moon rocks.

4. Collecting Moon Rocks

Geologists sometimes have difficulty collecting rocks on the earth. For example, they must from time to time travel in four-wheel drive jeeps through harsh, desolate areas, perhaps for days at a time. Or they might hike up and down steep, rugged mountainsides, lugging heavy backpacks filled with rock samples. It can be hard work—even if some of the mountainsides are in scenic places like the Rocky Mountains.

These problems are not serious, however, compared to those faced by geologists and other scientists who wanted to collect moon rocks. It simply is not easy to pick up rocks from a place that has no air and is located 238,000 miles away!

Special spacecraft had to be developed, built, and tested. Astronauts had to learn how to fly the spacecraft to the moon— and safely back to earth again. And to make the trip all the more worthwhile, the astronauts had to learn about geology so they would be prepared to collect rocks.

Astronauts' Flight Training

The astronauts' most important responsibility was to fly their spacecraft to the moon and back to earth again. For that reason, most astronauts were outstanding jet-aircraft pilots. In fact, the first astronauts were experienced test pilots—flyers who take to the air in new types of airplanes to see if they work right. Neil Armstrong, the first moonwalker, was considered to be one of the best test pilots in the world.

The astronauts practiced every aspect of a moonflight: countdown on the launching pad at the Kennedy Space Center in Florida, the two-day trip to the moon, lunar landing, takeoff from the moon, the blazing re-entry into the earth's atmosphere, and splashdown into the ocean. They even practiced how to climb out of the Apollo spacecraft as it bobbed up and down in the waves.

To test their skill at flying the lunar module, which is what NASA engineers called the spacecraft that would land on the moon, the astronauts used a *simulator*. A simulator is a computer-controlled machine that looks to the person in it to be a real spacecraft—but it never leaves the ground. The astronauts could look out the windows and see the moon's rough surface "below" them. They were not actually flying over the moon's surface, however. They were in a building at the Manned Spacecraft Center (now the Johnson Space Center) in Houston, Texas. Their view of the moon was made by projecting pictures (taken on previous space missions) of the moon onto screens surrounding the make-believe lunar module.

During the practice landings, NASA engineers would purposely create emergencies for the astronauts to correct. The problems were those that might (but hopefully would not) occur during an actual landing. The earthbound astronauts frequently

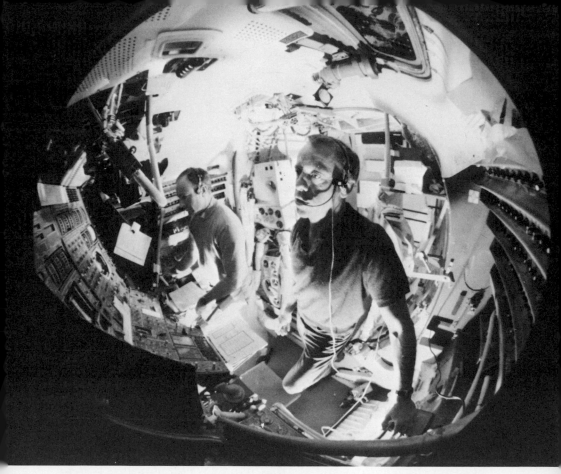

Astronauts Alan Shepard and Ed Mitchell in the lunar module simulator, practicing a lunar landing.

failed to solve the problems and "crashed" into the moon during their practice landings in the simulator. But better then, when safely on the ground in Houston, than when trying to land on the moon.

Astronauts' Geology Training
Except for Harrison H. Schmitt, who had a doctorate in geology from Harvard University, none of the astronauts who walked on

Astronauts Fred Haise (left) and Ed Mitchell collecting volcanic rock samples in Arizona.

the moon were geologists. An important part of their training, therefore, was a thorough course in geology.

The astronauts were trained by geologists from the United States Geological Survey and from NASA. The scientists taught their astronaut-students how to identify the most abundant types of rocks and minerals on the earth. They also traveled around the world to visit geological formations like those the astronauts might encounter on the moon. They visited large meteorite-impact craters in Arizona and Germany, and volcanic lava flows in Hawaii and the southwestern United States.

The astronauts practiced collecting rock samples in exactly the same way they would on the moon. They wore bulky back-packs like they would on the airless surface of the moon, took pictures of the rocks before and after chipping off a piece, and drove their electric dune-buggy (the lunar roving vehicle, or

Apollo 16 astronauts John Young (seated in the Rover) and Charles Duke prepare to collect rocks near Flagstaff, Arizona.

Apollo 14 astronauts Ed Mitchell and Alan Shepard practice setting up the instruments they would later set up on the moon.

Rover for short) from one sampling site to the next.

To fully imitate the actual collecting on the moon, the astronauts would even be in radio contact with NASA engineers in Houston. After selecting a rock to collect, an astronaut would describe the rock's color, shape, hardness, minerals present, and any other features he could see. The geologists who were teaching him would then check his description and point out the errors, if there were any.

A Trip to the Moon

From over three miles away, thousands of spectators could see the Saturn V rocket standing on the massive steel and concrete launching pad at the Kennedy Space Center in Florida. The Apollo spacecraft, with three busy but excited people aboard, was perched on top of the rocket, over 330 feet (100 meters) above the ground.

"One minute and counting," a man announced over a loudspeaker.

The countdown continued. Engineers and computers checked the rocket's many complicated systems to be sure all were operating properly.

"Thirty seconds and counting."

The spectators became quieter, yet more excited.

"Ten, nine, eight, seven, six, five, four, three, two, one . . ."

An enormous cloud of smoke and orange flame burst from the bottom of the Saturn V rocket, accompanied by a gigantic roar. The flaming rocket stayed on the ground for a few seconds, held by a steel arm. The arm fell away and the tall, sleek space-

Apollo 15 astronauts James Irwin, Al Worden, and Dave Scott arrive at the launch pad.

ship rose slowly and smoothly, gaining speed each second, heading for the blue sky above and the darkness of space beyond.

The astronauts inside were busy reading dials that told them their rocket was operating correctly. As they gained speed, the

Nighttime launch of Apollo 17, the last manned mission to the moon.

acceleration pushed them back in their seats. All the training, the practice, and the hard work had paid off. They were on their way to the moon.

Two days after blasting off the earth, Apollo was circling, or orbiting, around the moon. The spacecraft was about 60 miles (100 kilometers) above the moon's cratered surface.

The Apollo spacecraft consisted of three parts: the command

module, the service module, and the lunar module. The astronauts rode in the command module. The service module contained a small power plant that provided electricity to the command module. It also carried a camera and several scientific instruments. Most importantly, it contained the rocket engine that would send the spacecraft on its way back home.

Two astronauts boarded the lunar module, or LM (pronounced "lem"), through a tunnel, leaving the third crew member alone in the command module. The LM would separate from the rest of the Apollo spacecraft and descend to the lunar surface. While two astronauts worked on the moon, the third would be running a series of important experiments and taking photographs from orbit.

The LM was separated from the command module. After making sure that their spacecraft was operating properly, the astronauts fired the LM's rocket engines for about 30 seconds. This began the first phase of the descent to the moon's surface. The LM gradually decreased its altitude. After about an hour, the rockets were fired again. This was the "powered descent" phase and the rockets stayed on until landing, about 12 minutes later.

After gently touching down on the moon, the crew began to check out their spacecraft, making sure it was not damaged during the landing. When satisfied, they usually rested or ate a snack, preparing for the next part of the trip—collecting moon rocks and setting up a number of scientific experiments. They would finally get to use their geologic training.

The mission commander stepped out of the LM first. To insure

Apollo 16 astronaut John Young saluting the flag. In the background Stone Mountain rises 1,500 feet (300 meters) above the plain.

that the mission would return at least some lunar samples, he immediately opened a storage area, took out a shovel and dug it into the moon dirt. He placed the scoop of dirt, called the "contingency sample," into a plastic bag.

His partner then joined him and they set up a United States

flag. The flag was mounted on a pole with stiff wires so it appeared to be waving in the breeze, even though the airless moon has no wind.

Their first major job was to set up a scientific station not far from the LM. One of the most important pieces of equipment they placed on the ground was a seismometer, a sensitive machine that would detect moonquakes and meteorite impacts. On the earth, seismometers tell geologists what the earth is like inside. Lunar scientists hoped to find out a lot about the inside of the moon.

There were six manned moon landings. The astronauts on the first three missions spent a total of only 19 hours exploring the

Astronaut Charles Duke picks up a moon rock.

moon, setting up experiments, and collecting rocks. And all this was within walking distance of the LM.

But starting with the fourth trip, Apollo 15, their visits were much longer, and they had a car, the Rover, to drive around in. The Rover was a great help to lunar exploration because it allowed the astronauts to cover a much greater area than they could on foot.

As the two astronauts explored the moon, they picked up samples of the soil and pieces of rock lying around on the surface. One of the favorite places for rock collecting was the rims of craters. The rocks there were dug up from below the surface when the crater formed. This gave geologists a look at rocks from as much as 200 meters below the ground that the astronauts were standing on.

They also selected rock samples from large boulders. Some of the boulders were the size of a school desk, others the size of a car. Some were as large as a house.

The explorers raked some areas of the moon's surface. It was not that they were cleaning up a mess or raking autumn leaves. Instead, they were collecting rocks the size of marbles or walnuts. The soil on the moon contains mostly tiny grains, but larger rocks are also present. By using a rakelike tool, the small particles fell through, leaving the larger ones on the rake. These samples proved to be very useful to scientists back on earth, who nicknamed them "rakes" or "walnuts." The astronauts, now covered with dark, dusty moon dirt, climbed into the LM. They left behind their car, tools, and the seismometers and other experimental equipment. It was time to leave the moon and join their fellow astronaut in the command module.

Jack Schmitt collecting rocks near a large boulder.

The takeoff from the moon required another countdown, but one not as complicated as their blast-off from earth. When the LM's rockets ignited, the little spacecraft sprung off the moon and raced toward a meeting with the command module—and the two-day trip back home.

Back Again on Earth—the Geologists' Work Begins

After entering the earth's atmosphere like a blazing meteor, the command module floated on three parachutes to a splashdown in the Pacific Ocean, usually within a mile of the planned landing spot. The astronauts were safely back on earth. Now geologists

Splashdown in the Pacific Ocean—back home again!

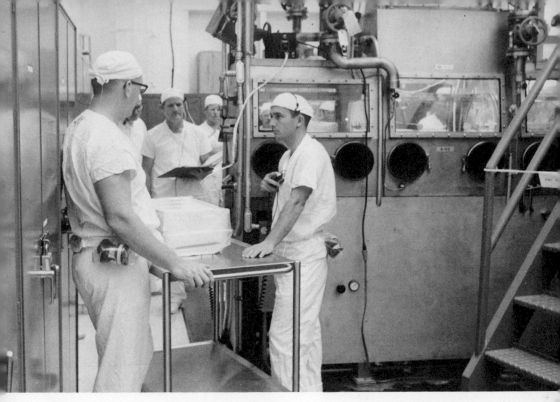

The first batch of moon rocks arrives in the Lunar Receiving Laboratory in Houston, Texas.

turned their attention to the rock and soil samples returned from the moon.

The samples, which had been stored in airtight cases, were removed from the command module and flown to the Lunar Receiving Laboratory in Houston. The cases were placed in glove boxes. These are glass and steel containers with windows and airtight rubber gloves attached. The glove boxes protected the rocks from air and dust.

The boxes also protected the scientists from the moon rocks— just in case dangerous germs lived on the moon. For the same reason, the astronauts were quarantined for three weeks when

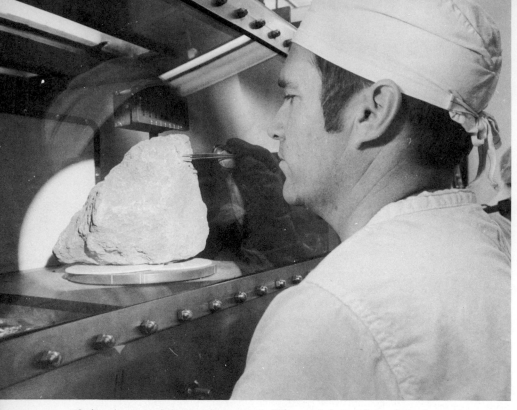

Scientist examining a moon rock. The rock is inside a glove box.

they returned to earth. No germs or other organisms were found, however.

After some tests were made on the samples, they were sent to scientists in the United States and fifteen other countries, including England, Australia, and West Germany. The scientists studied the rocks in every way possible. They found out what minerals and elements the rocks are made of, how old they are, and how they formed. They used the most modern equipment and techniques: mass spectrometers, electron microprobes, neutron activation, microscopes, and electron microscopes. They even took samples, heated and squeezed them in special apparatus,

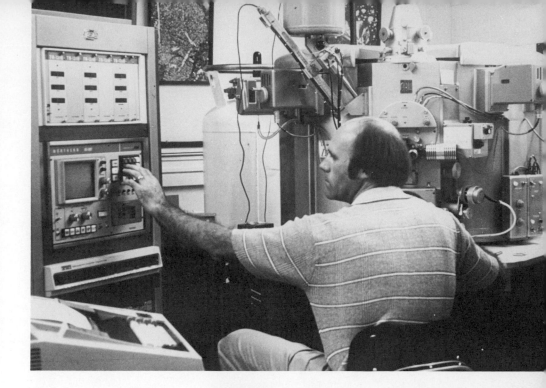

Above: *Geologist at the University of New Mexico using an electron microprobe to determine the chemical makeup of the minerals in a moon rock.*

Right: *This scientist at the Johnson Space Center in Houston, Texas, is adjusting the controls of equipment that heats and squeezes rock samples to temperatures and pressures like those inside the moon.*

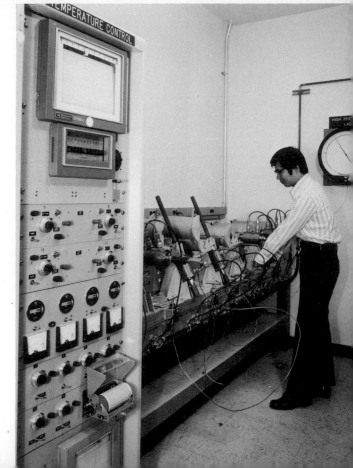

Scientists meet to discuss what they have discovered about the moon from their analyses of moon rocks.

trying to find out more about the rocks that exist inside the moon.

What did they find out? Plenty. They found out what the moon is made of, how old its rocks are, and its history. They even learned about a few of the events that took place during the earth's first half-billion years as a planet.

5. A Geologist's View of Moon Rocks

No Life, No Water

The geologists who studied the first batch of lunar samples returned by American astronauts made two important discoveries almost immediately. One was that nothing (and nobody) lives on the moon. The other discovery was that the moon does not contain water.

Before the lunar landings, of course, scientists knew that the moon was a barren place and that no large animals lived on it. However, once they made careful laboratory studies of the returned moon materials, they also learned that not even tiny, microscopic animals or plants live there. Biologists studying moon rocks and soils did not find a single bacteria, virus, or fungus.

Scientists used to wonder, before the manned landings, how much water the moon might have. They were sure there were no oceans or lakes present, but some features on the planet's surface, such as rilles, looked as though they might have been formed by water flowing downhill. Some geologists guessed that the moon may have had large bodies of water and big rivers millions of years ago, but that the water evaporated and was lost into space. So, before the Apollo landings, scientists asked the question, "How much water, if any, is there on the moon?"

Geologists determined the answer by searching for water in the moon rocks. The water would be present in certain minerals, such as mica, that form if water is present. No such minerals were found in any of the rocks or soils returned from the moon. The moon, therefore, contains no water, and it probably never did.

The geologists who analyzed the moon rocks also found out what the rocks are made of. There are three main kinds of rocks on the moon. One is found in the smooth mare areas; the other two occur in the mountainous highlands.

Stark, barren moon landscape.

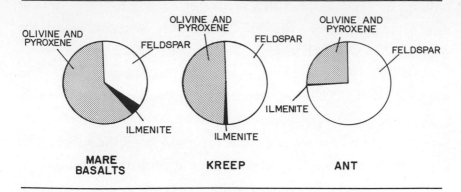

Percentages of minerals in the three main types of moon rocks.

Rocks from the Maria

The rocks occurring in the dark, smooth areas of the moon were once molten lavas. They resemble a type of rock known as basalt that geologists find in great abundance on the earth. The rocks that make up the mare areas of the moon are, therefore, called *mare basalts.* These once red-hot lunar lavas probably came up through long cracks, called fissures, in the moon's crust and flowed onto the surface. Volcanoes, however, like those found in Hawaii, the state of Washington, and many other places in the world, are rare on the moon.

Pieces of mare basalt look much like pieces of basalt from the earth. Most are dark gray or brownish gray. If you picked one up, you'd be able to see small, shiny crystals. Most of the crystals would be brownish, but many would be whitish, others would be black, and a few might be green. You would also see that the rock had numerous holes on its surface. Most of these holes are frozen gas bubbles that were present in the lava before it crystallized to solid rock. Basalts on the earth also have these holes

61

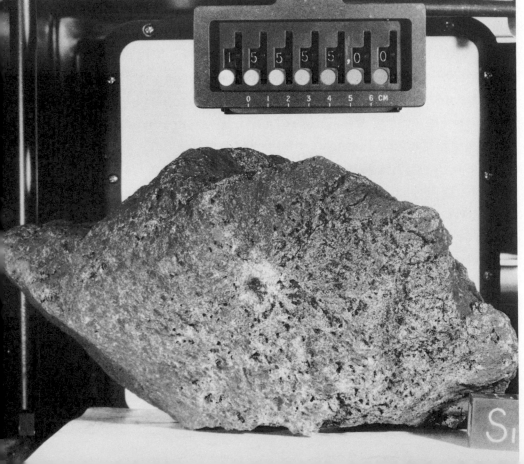

(called *vesicles*) in them. If you looked closely at the holes in a moon rock, some of them would look different from the rest. In fact, you might even say that they looked like small craters, which is what they are—tiny craters made by fast-moving meteorites smaller than a grain of sand. Geologists refer to these little craters in rock surfaces as *zap pits*.

The mare basalts differ in chemical composition from the rocks that make up the moon's highlands. The difference is most easily seen by comparing the abundances of the four most common minerals in lunar rocks. (All rocks, whether from the earth or moon, are made up of several different minerals. A mineral is a naturally occurring solid material that has a definite chemical composition and internal arrangement of its atoms.) These four important minerals in moon rocks are olivine, pyroxene, feldspar, and ilmenite. Olivine and pyroxene contain the elements iron, magnesium, and silicon. Feldspar contains calcium, sodium, aluminum, and silicon. And ilmenite is made of the elements iron and titanium. All four minerals also contain oxygen.

Mare basalts differ from other moon rocks by having more olivine and pyroxene than feldspar, and by containing sizable amounts of ilmenite. The mare basalts are not the same all over the moon, however, especially in the amount of ilmenite they contain. In those from the area where the Apollo 17 spacecraft landed, for example, ilmenite makes up about 20 percent of each rock, pyroxene 50 percent, and feldspar 30 percent. In another

Top left: *A gray and white boulder (about 1 meter across) at the Apollo 14 landing site.* Bottom left: *A sample of mare basalt collected by the Apollo 15 astronauts. Most of the holes are frozen gas bubbles, but the one in the center is a small crater called a zap pit.*

type of mare basalt, collected at the Apollo 12 landing site in the Ocean of Storms, ilmenite makes up only about 5 percent of each basalt, pyroxene 65 percent, and feldspar 30 percent. Geologists, however, consider these to be minor variations compared to the differences between mare basalts and the types of rocks found in the moon's rugged, mountainous highlands.

Rocks from the Highlands

Almost every rock collected from the highlands is a complex mixture of pieces of crushed rock and material that appears to have been molten. Geologists call such complicated rocks *breccias*. Some samples from the highlands are so complex that the crushed rock fragments they contain are themselves breccias.

What caused the formation of so many rocks with other rocks inside them? The most likely explanation is that meteorite impacts mixed different kinds of rocks together, crushing—and sometimes melting—them in the process. Every area in the highlands is covered with numerous craters, some of which are many miles across. The immense explosions caused by meteorites hitting the hard surface of the moon crushed and heated the rocks near the point of impact, forming a breccia. A second impact in the same spot mixed the first breccia into a second one, and so on. In this way, most of the rocks in the moon's heavily cratered highlands became complicated, rock-inside-rock breccias.

Two main types of rock occur in the highlands. Both contain more feldspar, hence more of the element aluminum, than mare basalts.

Scientists at the University of New Mexico nicknamed one of

An ANT rock collected by the Apollo 15 astronauts. The dark coating indicates that the rock was at one time inside another rock.

these rock types "ANT." This somewhat silly, but easy to remember, name comes from the first letters of three earth rocks (*a*northosites, *n*orites, and *t*roctolites) that are similar to the ANT rocks found on the moon. Feldspar makes up more than 75 percent of ANT rocks. Some samples, such as an Apollo 15 rock named the "Genesis Rock" by astronauts David Scott and

A complicated breccia of KREEP from the lunar highlands.

James Irwin, are made almost entirely of feldspar.

The other rock type found abundantly in the highlands also has a nickname: "KREEP." This unusual (and a bit creepy) name was invented by a group of geologists at the Johnson Space Center in Houston, Texas. It indicates that, compared to ANT rocks and mare basalts, KREEP rocks contain more potassium (whose chemical symbol is K), rare earth elements (abbreviated REE), and phosphorus (chemical symbol P). KREEP rocks are also different from mare basalts and ANT rocks in the amounts of feldspar, pyroxene, and ilmenite they contain, consisting of about 60 percent feldspar, 38 percent pyroxene, and only about 2 percent ilmenite.

The Ages of Moon Rocks

Scientists can determine a rock's age by measuring the abundances of certain radioactive elements. On the earth, the oldest rocks are about 3½ billion years old. Most, however, are far younger. In fact, some rocks, such as those erupting from volcanoes, are forming today.

On the moon, all the rocks are quite old. Mare basalts, the youngest of the moon rocks, range in age from about 3 billion years old to slightly less than 4 billion years old. None of the rocks returned by the Apollo astronauts is younger than 3 billion years. This indicates that the moon has been geologically dead for the past 3 billion years.

The moon almost certainly formed at the same time as the other planets, about 4½ billion years ago. Many scientists hoped that the rocks from the highlands would be as old as the moon itself. If so, careful study of the rocks might reveal clues that could help determine the origin of the moon. But surprisingly, when the rocks collected in the moon's highlands were dated, the oldest rocks were only about 4 billion years old, not the 4½ billion years everyone had hoped for. In fact, most of the ages were around 4 billion years, or slightly younger.

Why are there so few ages greater than 4 billion years? The answer seems to be that the meteorite impacts that formed the thousands of craters in the highlands and crushed and melted the rocks and made them into breccias, also reset the atomic clocks inside the rocks. The ages, therefore, represent the time that ANT and KREEP samples were involved in the formation of craters. The very large craters, such as the Mare Imbrium basin, formed during a period about 4 billion years ago when large meteorites bombarded the moon.

The Lunar Soil
Most soils on the earth are made of sand and clay particles mixed with plant and animal matter. Moon soils are nothing like that.

Moon dirt. Scientists removed grains smaller than 1 millimeter, leaving these larger pieces of rock. Markings on the little ruler are 1 millimeter apart.

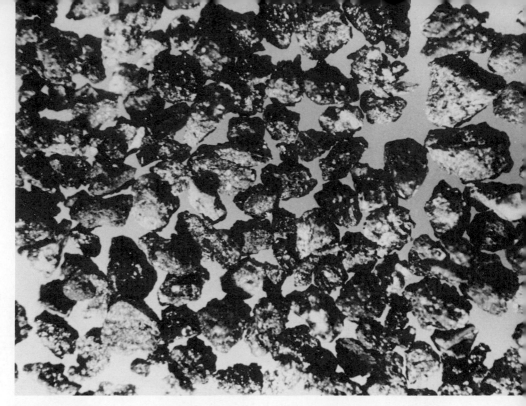

Scientists made this collection of small rock and mineral fragments by sieving a sample of moon soil. Largest fragments are 2 millimeters across.

Clay minerals contain water, so they cannot be present on the moon because the moon has no water. And since nothing lives or ever lived on the moon, lunar soils cannot contain the remains or waste products of plants or animals.

What, then, are moon soils like? Basically, the moon is covered with a thin layer of smashed-up rocks. This thin layer, called a *regolith*, averages 15 to 30 feet (5 to 10 meters) thick and covers the entire surface of the moon. Although the astronauts could see many boulders on the moon's surface, most of the regolith is made of pieces of rocks and minerals smaller than one millimeter (1/25 of an inch).

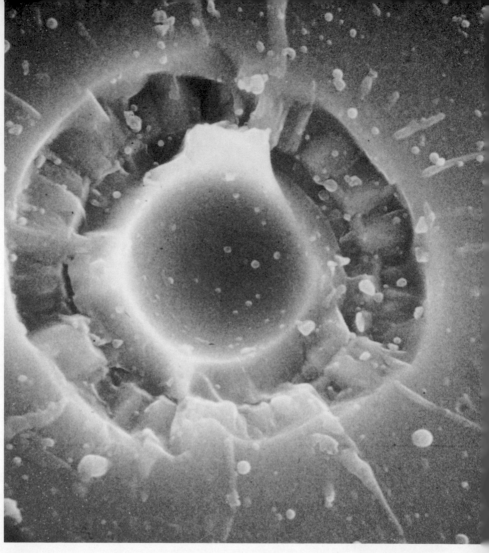

Zap pit, or microcrater, in a moon rock. The tiny crater, only 20 micrometers across, is smaller than the head of a pin. The photograph was made with a scanning electron microscope.

The rocks were smashed and battered by meteorite impacts during the past 3 or 4 billion years. Each meteorite that hit the moon broke up some more rocks. Many of the meteorites that crashed into the moon made large craters and, therefore, added numerous broken rocks to the surface. But most of the meteorites were not so large and so did not form large craters when they hit. In fact, some of them were so small that they made tiny craters in the surfaces of individual mineral grains in the soil. The smallest of these miniature craters, which geologists call microcraters or zap pits, are only 1/25,000 of an inch (1/1,000 of a millimeter) across. What a contrast to the crater Tycho, for example, which is 48 miles (87 kilometers) across—almost 100 billion times larger!

In addition to fragments of rock and minerals, the regolith also contains pieces of glass. When a meteorite hits the moon's surface, some of the rock it hits melts, and the melted material frequently squirts away as a small drop. These drops cool too fast to form minerals in them, so they end up as glass, which is simply

Thin slice of a lunar glass ball, as seen in a microscope. The ball is almost 1 millimeter across.

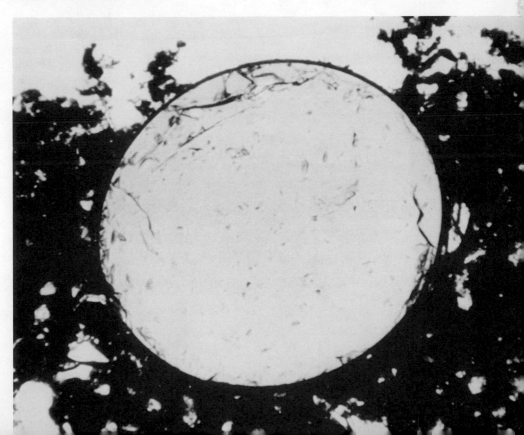

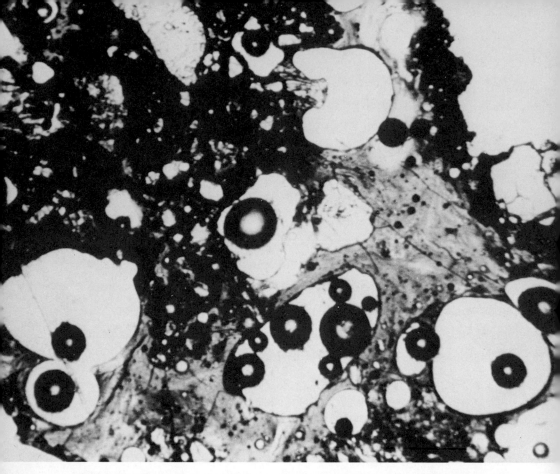

Thin slice through an agglutinate. Gray, swirly areas are glass. Dark areas are pieces of rocks and minerals. Clear areas are gas bubbles.

rocky material that did not crystallize. The lunar glasses come in a variety of bright colors, including orange, yellow, and green.

Sometimes a meteorite impact results in the formation of a new rock. One such rock is a soil breccia. An impact can press soil particles together and heat the compressed material. The combination of heat and pressure is enough to form a solid rock composed of all the other rocks and minerals and glasses pressed together. Another type of rock made in the regolith is called an *agglutinate*.

It forms when an impact melts some soil and then splashes the melt onto soil particles. The molten soil cools rapidly, forming a glass that holds the other soil particles together. Agglutinates are usually smaller than 1 centimeter, but they are very abundant in the regolith.

One of the most interesting and useful facts about the regolith is that a shovelful from one place contains pieces of rocks from all over the moon. Most of the fragments come from the rocks directly beneath, but because impacts throw rocks quite far, the regolith at any one spot receives material from all over. Thus, a soil in a maria is made of pieces of mare basalt, but it also contains fragments of ANT and KREEP rocks from the highlands. The opposite is true for the regolith in the highlands.

All Around the Moon

Apollo spacecraft landed at only six places on the moon, all on the nearside. Even with three samples obtained by unmanned landers sent by Russian scientists, that is not a very thorough investigation of the moon. How do we know if rocks other than mare basalts, ANT, and KREEP occur in large amounts elsewhere on the moon, particularly on the farside, where no spacecraft landed?

Lunar scientists are confident that no other types of rocks are present in great abundance on the moon. They even know that most of the moon's highlands, including those on the farside, are made of ANT rocks. They concluded this from studies of moon soils and from information obtained by a remarkable machine carried on the command module.

The regolith, or soil, that covers the moon is a mixture of the rocks under it and from farther away.

The soil at one place on the moon contains pieces of rock thrown there from faraway craters. Most of the soils dug up by the astronauts, therefore, contain at least a few rock samples from hundreds of kilometers away. If rocks different from mare basalts, ANT, and KREEP occur abundantly on the moon, scientists would have seen them in the moon soils—but none were found.

The Apollo 15 and 16 command modules carried two instruments that could measure the chemical composition of the moon's surface. Just as you can see color differences between the maria and highlands, these electronic marvels could "see" chemical differences. The chemical makeup of a rock or soil can be determined more accurately in a laboratory on earth, but these instruments were good enough to distinguish between mare basalts, ANT, and KREEP. They could also tell if another type of rock was present. Not bad for a machine located 60 miles (100 kilometers) above the moon!

As the electronic eyes peered down at the moon, they saw chemical differences. But the differences were in the amounts of mare basalts, ANT, and KREEP. No new rock types were found.

The one surprise is that the moon's farside is made almost entirely of ANT rocks. Mare basalts and KREEP rocks occur here and there, but they are not abundant. The moon, therefore, is lopsided: The nearside contains all three main rock types, but the farside is mostly ANT.

And Inside, Too
If it is a tricky business to find out what the surface of the moon is made of in places that were never visited, it is even more difficult to figure out what kind of rocks occur inside the moon.

This, of course, is no easier on earth. But by using sensitive instruments called seismographs, scientists have determined the structure of the earth's interior. The seismographs record the vibrations, called seismic waves, that travel through the earth from the site of an earthquake.

Apollo astronauts set up five seismometers on the moon. Except for the one set up during the Apollo 11 mission, which lost its

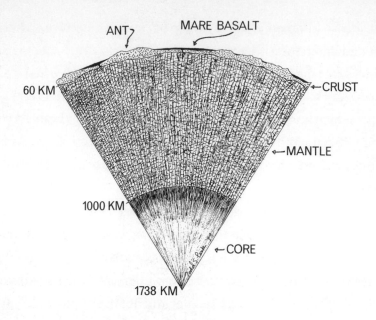

A view of the inside of the moon, showing the ANT crust, the mantle, and the partly liquid core.

power after only three weeks of operation, they operated continuously for several years.

From the vibrations produced by moonquakes and by meteorite impacts, scientists discovered that the moon has three main layers. The outer layer, or crust, starts at the surface and goes down to a depth of about 40 miles (60 kilometers). Since the velocity of the seismic waves in this outer layer is the same as it is in ANT rocks, scientists think that this layer is made mostly of ANT rocks. So not only are ANT rocks found all around the moon, they even extend to a depth of 40 miles.

Mare basalts occur on the surface, of course. But they do not form thick layers. Most maria contain a pile of basalts thinner

76

than a few kilometers. In many places, the mare basalts are less than one kilometer thick.

The layer beneath the ANT crust is the largest on the moon. It extends to a depth of 600 miles (1,000 kilometers). This layer, which most geologists call the mantle, does not resemble any of the rocks found on the surface. It is probably composed of olivine and pyroxene, with small amounts of feldspar and ilmenite.

The core of the moon begins at 600 miles and goes to the center, 1,090 miles (1,738 kilometers). This layer is unique because it seems to be at least partly molten. Scientists know this because one type of seismic wave, called an S-wave, disappears below 600 miles. Because S-waves do not travel through liquids, moonquake experts think that the center of the moon must be at least partly liquid, hence partly molten. They do not think, however, that the moon's core is made of iron and nickel, like the core of the earth is.

6. The Moon's Life Story

By studying moon rocks and using their imaginations and knowledge of geology, scientists figured out some amazing things about the moon. They determined, in fact, the moon's life story.

An Ocean of Magma

The first event in the moon's history took place when the little planet formed. A layer of molten rock (called magma) surrounded the entire moon. This ocean of magma, as many lunar scientists call it, was more than 125 miles (200 kilometers) deep. It must have glowed red-hot, like a gigantic lava flow.

How did geologists decide that this happened? ANT rocks gave them the clues.

The sizes and shapes of the crystals in some ANT samples told geologists that the rocks formed in a magma. But most rocks that form in this way are made of two or three, even four, main minerals, not one main mineral like ANT rocks. More than 75 percent of an ANT rock is feldspar. In fact, some ANT rocks are composed of almost nothing but feldspar. It took a special method to make these special rocks.

Feldspar, olivine, and pyroxene in the magma ocean may have behaved like toothpicks and pennies in a glass of water: feldspar may have floated to form the ANT crust and the heavier minerals may have sunk.

Geologists reasoned that feldspar, which is lighter than the other minerals in moon rocks, must have floated to the top of the pool of magma in which ANT rocks formed. As the feldspar floated, the heavier minerals sank.

You can get an idea of the process by doing a simple experiment. Get a glass of water and some pennies and wooden toothpicks. Throw the pennies and toothpicks into the water. The pennies, because they are heavier than the water, will sink, while the toothpicks will float.

Geologists think that feldspar floated to the top of the lunar magma to form ANT rocks. Olivine, pyroxene, and ilmenite sank to form layers at the bottom of the ocean of magma.

But why do geologists think it must have been an ocean of magma that surrounded the whole moon? Why not smaller pools of magma? The answers to these questions lie in knowing how much ANT rock there is on the moon and where it occurs.

The instrument that measured the moon's chemical composition from the orbiting command module indicated that ANT rocks occur all around the moon. Since ANT rocks are found everywhere, geologists reasoned that the magma ocean must have covered the entire moon.

Scientists guess that the ocean of magma was at least 125 miles (200 kilometers) deep. The seismometers set up on the moon by the Apollo crews showed that the moon's crust was about 40 miles (60 kilometers) thick and made mostly of ANT rocks. The ANT layer formed by feldspar floating to the top of the magma ocean. Other minerals had to sink at the same time.

Because scientists think it likely that there were more of the other minerals than feldspar, the thickness of the layer made by

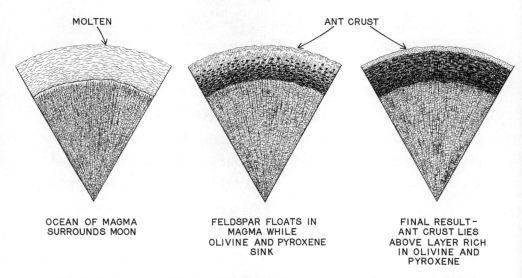

MOLTEN   ANT CRUST

OCEAN OF MAGMA   FELDSPAR FLOATS IN   FINAL RESULT–
SURROUNDS MOON   MAGMA WHILE   ANT CRUST LIES
                        OLIVINE AND PYROXENE   ABOVE LAYER RICH
                        SINK   IN OLIVINE AND
                                                    PYROXENE

The cooling and solidification of the ocean of magma that surrounded the moon when it formed.

Dome-shaped mountains called the Gruithuisen domes. The mountain with the small crater on top (center of photo) is 13 miles (20 kilometers) across and over 3,800 feet (1,200 meters) high. Scientists think these mountains are made of KREEP rock and are over 4 billion years old.

the sunken minerals was probably thicker than the one made by the floating feldspar. A good guess is that the sunken layer is three times thicker. Adding the thicknesses of the ANT and sunken layers results in a thickness of more than 125 miles. Some scientists speculate that the magma ocean may have been as much as 625 miles (1,000 kilometers) deep.

KREEPy Volcanoes

The second event in the moon's life took place when it was still fairly young. About 200 or 300 million years after the moon

formed, lavas flowed onto the surface and erupted from volcanoes. When the lavas cooled, they became the first KREEP
rocks. KREEP lavas continued to spurt out from volcanoes or
from long cracks (called fissures) until about 600 million years
after the moon formed, or slightly less than 4 billion years ago.

Although almost all ages determined for KREEP rocks indicate
that they are only about 4 billion years old, scientists learned
from complicated analyses of radioactive elements that KREEP
rocks began to form before that. Exactly when the first KREEP
lavas started to flow across the moon's surface is difficult to determine because the rocks were crushed, melted, and mixed up by
meteorite impacts soon after they formed.

Bombardment

The next stage in the moon's history took place about 4 billion
years ago and lasted about 100 to 150 million years—a short time
in the life of a planet. The moon was bombarded by millions of
meteorites, some of them many kilometers across. Craters were
made on top of craters. The rock thrown out by one impact was
soon thrown out again by another. Nobody was around to watch,
but it must have been an exciting fireworks display!

The evidence that the moon was the victim of this bombardment comes from observations of the heavily cratered highlands
and from the appearance of the rocks found there.

The highlands are covered with craters that frequently overlap
one another. Many craters are so covered with other craters
that you can barely see where they were. Others were undoubt-
edly completely erased by craters that formed on top of them.

Most of these craters in the highlands formed during the period of bombardment, about 4 billion years ago.

Because the explosions that blasted out the craters must have damaged the rocks in and around each one, it is no wonder that the rocks from the highlands are complicated, mixed-up, rock-inside-rock breccias.

The ages of ANT and KREEP rocks are around 4 billion years, but there is a slight spread in ages. The range is about 100 to 150 million years. This led scientists to conclude that the bombardment lasted about that long, up to 150 million years.

It was during this period that the large basins formed on the moon. As discussed, there are 43 basins larger than 220 kilometers across. These giant craters must have been made when enormous rocky objects struck the moon. Scientists estimate that the Mare Imbrium basin was created when a meteorite larger than the state of Rhode Island crashed into the moon.

Mare Basalts

As things calmed down on the lunar surface toward the end of the period of intense bombardment, the inside of the moon was heating up. The result was that more lavas oozed from the moon and flowed across its cratered surface. This time the lavas were mare basalts. Based on the ages of the returned samples, this period lasted from slightly less than 4 billion years ago to about 3 billion years ago.

The mare basalts made their way to the surface along cracks in the crust. The cracks were made, at least in part, by the impacts during the period of bombardment. When the lavas reached the surface, they flowed downhill and filled up the low areas. Because craters are low spots, these were the places where the

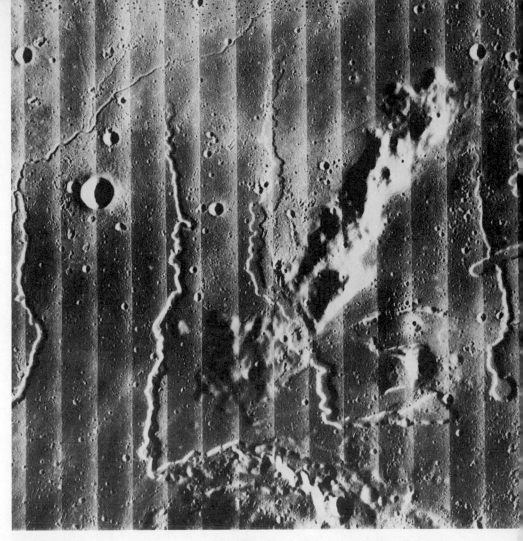

Smooth mare area with rilles. Mare basalts formed from about 4 billion to about 3 billion years ago.

lavas went. As a result, the large basins were filled with mare basalts, forming the great "seas" that splotch the moon's face and appear as the "Man in the Moon."

Lunar scientists are puzzled by the rarity of mare basalts on the moon's farside. There are just as many basins there, so why didn't the lavas erupt on the farside? The answer seems to be that the ANT crust is thicker on the farside than it is on the nearside. The mare basalts may not have reached the surface on the farside because there was too much crust to rise through.

Laboratory experiments with mare basalts indicate that they formed when solid rock heated up and began to melt. The melting took place over 60 miles (100 kilometers) below the lunar surface. The rocks that melted were made mostly of olivine and pyroxene—the *same* minerals that sank in the magma ocean when feldspar floated to form the ANT crust.

Mare basalts, therefore, formed in two steps: Olivine, pyroxene, and ilmenite sank in the ocean of magma that surrounded the young moon. Then, beginning about 4 billion years ago, these same minerals began to melt and make lavas that would rise to the surface and become mare basalts.

Geologically Lazy

Since the last mare basalts erupted onto the moon, about 3 billion years ago, the moon's geological machine seems to have worn out. The only melting takes place far in the interior, below a depth of 1,000 kilometers. This is too deep for the magmas to reach the surface.

Except for an occasional meteorite impact, the moon is geologically dead. It preserves the surface that existed 3 billion years ago.

It does, of course, still faithfully circle the earth and brighten the night sky. And it still makes us wonder about how it formed. Only now we know much of its history.

7. The Moon and the Earth

Although geologists still have a lot to learn about the earth and the moon, they have studied the two neighboring bodies better than any others in the solar system. They have examined rocks from the moon's maria and highlands, from the earth's continents and ocean floors. They even know a lot about the insides of each by studying earthquake and moonquake vibrations.

The moon and earth are similar in many respects. The same elements occur in each, although in different amounts. Rocks seem to be formed in the same ways on the moon as on the earth. And each planet is layered, having a crust, a mantle, and a core.

But there are some important differences between the earth and the moon.

The earth has a large iron-nickel core that is mostly liquid. The moon, in contrast, has only a small core and it may not be made of iron at all. It may only be partly molten rock.

The moon has been geologically inactive for 3 billion years. But the earth is anything but geologically dead. The *oldest* earth rocks are not much older than the *youngest* moon rocks. In fact,

The earth and moon are shown here in their true relative sizes, although they are much farther apart than they appear here.

rocks are forming right now, erupting from volcanoes in places like Hawaii, or being laid down in the ocean, or at the mouths of rivers like the Mississippi. Immense blocks of the earth, whole continents in fact, are moving around, colliding and causing earthquakes and volcanoes. Rain pours from the sky and erodes the rocks. The earth is a restless planet, continuously making and destroying mountains. The moon is asleep.

The moon contains no water. What a contrast to the earth, where oceans cover 75 percent of the surface. The earth also has a protective, life-giving layer of air surrounding it. The moon has no air.

The restless, wet earth is also alive with people, animals, and plants. It has red, yellow, white, purple, and pink flowers. Short grasses and giant redwood trees. Fish, whales, crabs, bears, lions, tigers, and the family dog. And it has people who work, play, and think. People who invent, explore, and wonder—wonder about the moon, the earth, and how the planets formed.

The moon contains no form of life.

The Earth's Story—As Told by the Moon

The earth is so geologically active that we do not know much about its early history. The oldest earth rocks are about 3 ½ billion years old, but these are quite rare. Since scientists must understand all of earth history to fully understand how the planet works now, they must know what happened 3 ½ billion years ago.

Perhaps the moon knows what took place on the earth. Many scientists think that the earth's first 500 to 600 million years of

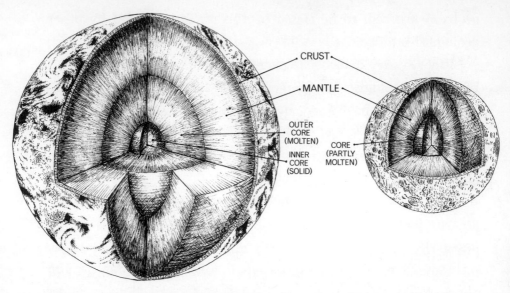

CRUST

MANTLE

OUTER
CORE
(MOLTEN)

INNER
CORE
(SOLID)

CORE
(PARTLY
MOLTEN)

The insides of the moon and the earth are similar in some ways, but different in others.

life were similar to the moon's. If so, then we know at least some of the events that took place on the young earth.

When our planet formed, it may have been surrounded by an immense ocean of magma. The magma ocean on the moon was about 200 kilometers deep, but the one on the earth may have been much deeper. This event probably led to the formation of the main layers of the earth, including the iron core and the rocky mantle.

Scientists are not sure what happened after the earth's magma ocean began to cool and solidify. There may have been numerous volcanoes and water may have started to fill the oceans. However, it seems likely that the earth was bombarded by millions of meteorites, just as the neighboring moon was. Immense basins probably formed, to be erased by further impacts and by other geological activity.

Little, if any, evidence remains of the earth's bombardment. However, geologists are examining the oldest rocks on earth to see if they may have been involved in cratering events. Even if all record of this period of the earth's history is lost, just knowing that it may have happened is useful to geologists trying to unravel the early history of the earth.

After the basins formed on the earth, they may have been filled with basalts. Geologists are looking for clues that would prove that this happened. It is a difficult search because rocks that formed nearly 4 billion years ago have been heated up and changed in their appearance since then.

The search goes on for direct evidence that the earth had an ocean of magma, was bombarded, and then erupted basalts onto its surface to fill the scars left by the bombardment. Geologists are using their knowledge of the moon, a little planet 238,000 miles away, to help us understand how the earth began and what happened on it while it was still a young planet. It is a difficult, but fascinating search.

Index

93

About the Author

G. Jeffrey Taylor is a senior research scientist in the Department of Geology and Institute of Meteoritics at the University of New Mexico. He is a native of New York and received his bachelor's degree from Colgate University in 1966 and his Ph.D. from Rice University in 1970. G. Jeffrey Taylor has been involved in research on lunar samples since 1970 and has contributed more than fifty articles about moon rocks and meteorites to scientific journals. This is his first book for children.